Could You Be Love?: Poems & Prayers Dedicated to the 8 Types of Love

Brittnee Wilder

BookLeaf Publishing

India | USA | UK

Could You Be Love?: Poems & Prayers
Dedicated to the 8 Types of Love © 2024
Brittnee Wilder

All rights reserved.

No part of this publication may be
reproduced, stored in a retrieval system, or
transmitted, in any form or by any means,
electronic, mechanical, photocopying,
recording or otherwise, without the prior
written permission of the presenters.

Brittnee Wilder asserts the moral right to be
identified as author of this work.

Presentation by *BookLeaf Publishing*

Web: www.bookleafpub.com

E-mail: info@bookleafpub.com

ISBN: 9789358315509

First edition 2024

To God, my source and strength to keep pushing because it is all possible through him. To my parents who planted the seeds of knowledge and gave me a true love for education and writing at an early age. For my daughter, who showed me the real meaning of unconditional love. To my closest friends, family, and village that consistently poured into me while completing this book. To ALL the lovers who will read this book, keep believing in your love story. I promise it is coming! Until it comes, be present and enjoy each and every part of your journey.

ACKNOWLEDGEMENT

To anyone I gave my energy,time,effort, and genuine love to. First off, thank you for your contribution to my experience in learning what love truly is. A personal thank you to anyone that broke my heart. You taught me a very valuable lesson and that is: Time can and will heal it all if you decide you want to heal. My success in love has been just as important as my failures. A huge shout out to God who took my broken heart and mended it over and over again without any judgment!

PREFACE

Could You Be Love? Is a book filled with poems and prayers about the 8 different types of love. It is one woman's experience as love has helped her grow, taught her tough lessons,and helped her heal. Each and every poem and prayer is specific to the situation and the outcomes of each experience. It is the honest and real conversations of the heart after pain and hurt have occurred. It is the beautiful words of encouragement and love from family, friends, and children. Overall this book was created to help inspire people through their heartbreak to heal and to allow love to find them right where they are in this life.

Damn! I Look Good

I bought a new dress the other day.
It showed off my curves just in the right way.
It rolled off my hips,
Just like fingertips.
Sophisticated talk,
Lovely walk with a twist.
Beautiful, Black, Diva walking in one hell of a
dress no one can resist.
This woman can get
any man she sets
her eyes upon.
No games , gimmicks, or a con.
Something like the female Don Juan…
Breezing through my haters with my head held
high.
Smiling at the whistles, the "Oooooo's", and the
sighs.
And this is me on a day that I didn't even try…
Damn...I ….Look GOOD!

My prayer for you is that on the days where you
don't feel your best that you still show up for

yourself. That you can look at this poem and be inspired that you are THE IT FACTOR! Even on your worst of days, you have something so amazing inside of you. I pray that God comforts you through whatever you are going through right now. That you can love yourself throughout the different challenges you face in the world. My biggest prayer is that you don't let one bad day turn into a bad month or a bad year. It's okay to take a day off, rest, reset, and start again.

Amen,

B. Wilder

Journey to Self Love

In the quiet chambers of this heart,
Where echoes whisper, a brand-new start.
An inner journey, a sacred quest,
Discovering the love that you possess.

Embrace the mirror, behold your reflection,
A masterpiece, a unique connection.
In the canvas of your being, colors bloom,
A symphony of self, a sweet perfume.

Celebrate the pieces that make you whole,
The scars, the laughter, the stories untold.
For within your essence, is where treasure lies,
A radiant glow that never denies.

Gentle whispers of self-compassion,
Softly echo, a tender confession.
Love thyself, with arms wide open,
A song of grace where no judgment is spoken.

Cast out doubt with a confident smile,
A journey of self-love,mile by mile.
Let self-love be your guiding star,
Illuminating who you truly are.

My prayer for you is that you really invest in
your self love journey for YOU! That you don't
just do self love because it's a fad, but that you
really use it as a way to know thyself. I pray you
understand that in order to really receive the
love you truly desire, you have to give that love
to yourself first.I pray you take your self love
journey one day at a time and get excited about
discovering the special things about you. It is
true you are unique and there is no one on this
earth that is exactly like you. I pray you embrace
your differences and love you for who you are.

Amen,
B.Wilder

Who Am I?

I am from incense burning of a a soft musk scent

from Africa's Best Herbal Oil on my legs &
Luster's Pink Lotion on my Kinky hair

I am from The Hilltop "2321 S. 16th Street" to
be exact where "It better be cleaned before I get
home"

I am from Palmer's Cocoa butter on every cut,
burn, or blister whose healing power brought
back that Black Natural Beauty

I am from my dear diary and rocking Mom's old
pager like it was actually activated

from the Thompson's Diabetes to the Harris's
high blood pressure

I am from back breaking work until the day we
die and musically talented on any given Sunday

and from laughing about it or else I'm gonna cry

from sticking together because that's what
siblings do

I am from "If you were able to go out last night,
you're able to get up and get to church in the
morning" or "God gives his toughest battles to
his strongest soldiers"

I am from Ellen & Ruth from Hot Tamale Pie
and Collard Greens with Cornbread

from moving from Texas to Washington in order
to create our family legacy, our church

from singing "I'm a little Teapot short and stout"
in front of family for dollars

I am from those moments where you realize you
don't get to choose your family, you just love
them anyhow

My prayer for you is that you never forget where
you come from as you continue to move forward
in this life. That you honor yourself, your family,

and your city. I pray you recognize that you provide so much inspiration to others by simply being yourself. People are watching you closely and see the way you handle things. You help them to want to do and be better. The way you bounce back from some of life's toughest situations is truly motivational. Your strength and grit is beautiful. I pray you keep going and push forward for you!

Amen,
B. Wilder

Sister-Friend

Your sisterhood has changed me.

It has made me realize that I don't have to do it all alone.

It showed me that I'm not the only one who is crazy.

Those calls with heartfelt advice have enhanced my life.

The times in my single season when all I needed was quality time with my friend, you showed up faithfully.

You have supported me in ways that others would never.

The impromptu sleep overs.

The safe space to yell, scream, and cry.

The hugs that are right on time.

Pure acceptance, without any judgment.

Correction with love.

Your understanding without pointing the finger.

Then the encouragement to keep going for the life I deserve.

Our spiritual conversations that confirm God's alignment for our friendship.

I could never thank you for everything, but just know that this bond is priceless.

My prayer is that you find a strong core group of friends that will hold it down for you in this life. That they hold you accountable and you do the exact same for them. I pray your friends are a good fit for your life. That they encourage you when you are feeling at your lowest. I pray for a friend group that sees the potential in you and will kindly let you know that you can do better in whatever capacity you are settling in. I pray that you have friends that will grow and mature

with you so that you will have long lasting
friendships. That God sends you friends with
genuine hearts and intentions within your
friendship. My biggest prayer is for positive
energy exchanges between you and your truest
tribe. That you find a group of friends that you
fit right in without even having to try.

Amen,

B.Wilder

Sisterly Yours

My heart has a special place for Z PHI B.
And yes it's THE BEST Sorority.
Especially to ALL of my Sisters too.
Who look good in the purest white and royal
blue.

A Zeta woman is a finer woman.
A woman who is always headed towards more
success.
Who has been through some things in life,
But recognizes that she is more than blessed.

See, my Sorors are good Zetas.
Who are well informed Zetas.
Bold women who give to the world the best they
have.
Humbled ladies, who never ever have to brag.

Not only is a 1920 Lady going to look amazing.
But, she demands attention in any room she
steps in
She doesn't even need to try
You are simply drawn to her when you look in
her eye

No matter what you look like or how your hair
should curl
There is a Zeta in each and every little girl.
If you are searching for her, just look at her blue
light that constantly shines.
She is the Finer woman in the royal blue and
isn't hard to find.

Lets not forget about the bonds and
relationships.
Connection to Our 5 Pearls and genuine
friendships
The songs we sing loud with so much pride
The laughs that are shared and tears that are
cried.

Zeta Business and Social Events aren't up for
debating.
There is a true balance in everyone participating.
Keep in mind Zeta doesn't mind stepping or
strolling,
Because there is no way to stop this Zeta train
from rolling.

My prayer is that you fall in love with a cause
that is bigger than yourself. That you align
yourself with like minded people who have
similar hearts to serve their community in
multiple ways. I pray you are intentional about
creating and maintaining sisterhood and
friendships. That you focus on the business
aspect and also the fun aspect of your
organization. That you find a healthy balance as
you maneuver through your organization. I pray
you feel loved and welcomed at all times. I also
pray that you become adventurous and discover
things for yourself.My biggest prayer is that
your create so many beautiful memories with the
group you align with.

Amen,
B.Wilder

Dearest Daughter

Baby Girl,

I'd give you the world and all of its riches.

Teach you that BLACK women are the truest queens,not BITCHES.

Explain to you that the way you carry yourself in public is how you choose to be seen.

Give you understanding that life is nothing without genuine happiness,it's not always about the green.

Show you how to defend yourself in times of disrespect.

Instruct you on how to drive the right way and keep you out of a wreck.

I'd tell you about my mistakes in relationships and hope you'd listen and learn.

Show you that revenge isn't worth it and the other cheek is what you should turn.

Preach to you about what real music is and then turn around and listen to your music too.

Ask you about all the things and trust that you'll always be true.

Show you how to sing like Mommy.

Then attempt to show you how to dance like Daddy.

Act crazy when you're with your friends.

Especially when it's with me and your father.

Just know that these things are out of love unconditionally because you are my daughter.

-Mommy loves you

My prayer is that you feel beautiful and confident at all times. That you are bold and brave when fear tries to creep in. I pray that you trust and understand the power of your voice. That you stay curious in your journey of self

discovery and self love. I especially pray that
you love yourself more than anyone else could.
That you recognize that no matter what you are
valuable even if someone else doesn't see it for
themselves.My biggest prayer is for you to live
an amazing and long lasting life. A life filled
with fun,adventurous, and breathtaking
moments.

Amen,
B.Wilder

Letter to Mom (It Never Fully Goes Away)

Hey Mom,

I thought about you today as I often do.
Realizing more than ever how much I look like
you, talk like you,and just have your infectious
laughter.
I hear you in my thoughts, your many sayings
stick with me, and your same love for music is
deeply rooted in my soul.
Some days are harder than others, but there are
days where I can keep my emotions in control.
It's crazy how sometimes it feels like it's been 9
years.
Then other days it feels like it's only been 9
minutes since you left.
Grief is funny that way.
You can work on healing grief, but it never fully
goes away.
They say that with time it gets better, but I wish
someone would've told me it's all about what
you do with that time.
If you choose healing and actually work towards
it then you will be fine.

I replay your famous words "I'll always be in
your heart" in my head.
That always helps me dodge the tears and rest in
our beautiful memories instead.

My prayer for you is that you work through your
grief. I pray for healing and strength. If you have
lost a parent I pray for your broken heart. I pray
you feel the presence of God as you walk
through your grief journey. My prayer is that
you have a big and beautiful support system that
you can lean on as you go through such a tough
transition of losing a parent.I pray that you hold
on to God's hand as you go through the stages of
grief and that you know eventually there will be
a place of peace and acceptance that you come
into. I pray that once you reach that point that if
other friends and family go through similar
situations that you are able to hold their hand
through their journey as well. That you give
yourself grace and are kind to yourself each step
of the way. That you don't put any expectations
on yourself to do things that you might have
been able to do easily before grief. My biggest
prayer is that you take it one day, one hour, one
minute, or even one second at a time. Take a

deep breath and just take one step. You got this
and God has you!

Amen,
B.Wilder

In Fact-uation

I'd risk it all just to be close.
Intimacy was what I always desired the most.
Somewhere in the midst of forced feelings and
forced relationships.
Pretending like our bond was heaven sent.
When I know damn well you were sent just to
distract me.
To keep my mind so far on you, that I'd forget
about what's next for me.
I'd be too busy replaying our conversations over
in my mind,
Or stuck on the hugs you gave me from behind.
Too preoccupied by the butterflies in my
stomach that appear,
Every single time I hear,
Your deep baritone voice.
I am completely enticed by you,
almost like I don't have a choice.
I'm paralyzed,
when you rub on my thighs.
And we can call it a done deal if you decide to
kiss me,
With the softest lips on the planet.
Can't you see that I'm already yours?
Then why wouldn't you lean into me?

Haven't I shown you I'm fun, loyal, completely
obsessed, and only about you?
I have to release myself from this illusion of
how I thought this would be.
I really thought that once you knew my heart,
you'd be all about me.
But see, that's it!
I forgot to play the game and run the race.
How foolish of me to think that I was in first
place.
When I know now I'm just second string,
A fling.
That's exactly what we were.
Although it was all a game for you, my
intentions were pure.

My prayer for you is that you recognize the
difference between people who are godly divine
relationships and those that are sent as
distractions. That you recognize quickly when
someone is for you as opposed to being all about
themselves. I pray that you notice all the little
things that make you feel some type of way
when you are with them. That you pay attention

to your energy after you are done being with
them. My biggest prayer is that you are not
tricked by loneliness or codependency to be with
somebody just to be with somebody. My hope is
that you learn to walk away from anyone that
causes you anxiety,worry, or obsession. I pray
you consult with God/Source about anyone who
shows interest in you.I also pray that you stay in
the present and you don't allow the illusions of
what you could be to clutter your brain. That
you don't fall in love with the potential ,but that
you pay attention to what actually is. Take
everything for face value and pay attention to
the actions way more than the words.I pray that
you ultimately use your discernment to
determine if this person is good for you or not.

Amen,
B.Wilder

Use Me

I wanna be used by YOU, but when I say used.
No. no. I don't mean abused, but hear me out
right quick.
I mean used.
Used like your favorite pair of shoes,
Or your lucky hat.
The one that you wear back to back.
I'm talking about used, like your very first car.
You know the one that got you safely from a to z
or near and far.
Used. Used.
Like your favorite saying in the middle of a
conversation with your A1 Day1.
It would give me nothing, but pure pleasure to
simply be USED.
Like your favorite sibling's hand me downs.
Use me again and again and around and around.
Like use me as your favorite dessert.
You know the one you lick ALL the icing off
before you eventually nibble right in my middle.
JUST...LIKE...THAT...
Baby only you can USE me.
Like you use that Jack and Coke
…and let my sweet nectar slide all the way
down your throat.

Smoke.
But of course you can use me when you smoke.
Puffing on my swisher sweets, but don't you
dare choke.
I love being used like an instrument.
Just pluck each and every one of my strings and
listen to the heavenly hums that escape this
hurricane tongue.
Keep using each and every part of my body as
your personal possession.
That only you cherish.
Use me baby until there isn't anything left.
Because to be used by you is what I was made
for.
So feel free to use me more and more.

My prayer is that you recognize your worth and
value at all times. That you give your all to
someone who is willing and able to give their all
to you as well. I pray that your relationships are
a two way street and that nothing is one-sided.
My biggest prayer is for you to find someone
who is in alignment with you physically,
emotionally, mentally, sexually, and spiritually.

That you do not settle for someone who is not
what you actually want. That you make a
decision to be single if it comes down to you
choosing someone who is close to everything
you want. That you recognize that entertaining
someone who is not it is keeping you from the
one who is for you. I pray you have the courage
to cut off situationships that won't even matter
once the one for you comes along. That you
invest all your energy and time into yourself
until you find someone who is worthy of all you
have to offer.

Amen,
B.Wilder

Confusing Love

After the ecstasy what's left?
Only the resentment, agony, and pain.
No "I love yous" or cuddling.
Just you in your area and me in mine.
Our paths will never be crossed by each other
again… UNLESS?
No!No!No!
You can't keep doing this to me.
I can't keep doing this to myself.
I will end this.
Hell, I already have.
My heart is just being hard headed.
It keeps going back and forth, so unsure of its
permanent home,
But the best thing for me to do is to leave you
alone.
The whole situation,stuck in a conversation with
my heart and soul.
One asks the other "Why is it so hard for you to
let him go?"
I think it's because when I'm done with someone
it's done forever.
And I honestly can't say that we won't get back
together.
All we've done is constantly spin the block.

It's time for one of us to grow the fuck up and stop.
So here it goes: (sigh) GOOD-BYE.

My prayer for you is that you recognize that you are so worthy of someone who is willing to go all in to be with you. That you understand that the one for you will never be lukewarm about you, but they will be on fire for you.I pray you realize quickly when they are not the one and you feel confident enough to move forward. That you don't get caught up in the feelings of loneliness and go back over and over again.I pray you don't get stuck in the toxic culture of spinning the block because it is emotionally exhausting.I pray God gives you clarity before you decide to spin the block for someone who wouldn't even cross the sidewalk for you. Remember you are worthy of someone who would put you first each and every time. Hang onto this thought and stay strong!

Amen,
B.Wilder

Toxic Ties

In shadows deep where pain resides,
An adventure starts, where hope abides.
From toxic bonds, we have to break the chain,
And Embrace healing's gentle rain.

Inside the heart, scars etched in time,
A wounded soul, a paradigm.
But courage blooms, a flower bright,
To seek the dawn, end the night.

The memories of a love gone completely wrong,
A haunting melody, a mournful song.
Yet through the trauma, strength will emerge,
As healing covers, a soft surge.

From ashes rise, a spirit free,
Reclaiming self, identity.
No longer tethered, broken wing,
But soaring high, a song to sing.

The damage remain, but stories tell,
Of resilience, a magic spell.
For in the healing, strength is found,
A brighter self, love unbound.

So celebrate this day, reborn,
A year has passed since love was torn.
From toxic chains, you've been set free,
A wiser heart, a jubilee.

My prayer is that you are able to steer clear of
the toxic ties you've created. That you will value
yourself better than they ever did. I pray that you
recognize that your toxicity is not good for
either one of you. That you understand that self
love has always been the goal. I pray you know
now that if you can't love yourself
unconditionally, then you cannot expect anyone
else to love you unconditionally. The way we
treat and love ourselves shows others how to
treat and love us as well. Make sure you are
giving yourself the most love. My hope and
prayer is that you understand that you have the
power to change your mind at any moment .So
feel free to use your power when needed.

Amen,
B.Wilder

A Short Lived Unforgiveness

The pressure has been released and the weight
lifted off the shoulders.

But the hurt still remains.

Regret,Shame, and Bitterness live in the soul.

They are the emotional boulders

That declines the healing waters to flow.

We may be officially over, but thoughts of you
stay inside this mind.

Struggling to let go and peace is hard to find.

Secret prayers whispered in the middle of the
night.

With the desired hope to find my Mr. Right.

My prayer is that the hurt,pain, and trauma you
went through in that last relationship doesn't
stay in your heart. I pray that you recognize that
forgiveness is the greatest gift you can give
yourself. That you work out a way to heal so that
you can be open to the one who truly wants to
love you and treat you right. My biggest prayer
for you is that you don't block your blessings by
being so concerned or stuck in your past. That
you realize that the past is in the past because
it's time to get past it! All you can do is be and
do better as you move into your future. I pray
you trust that God has something bigger and
better for you.That each failed relationship was
simply a lesson for you to learn and apply so
that you can become the person God is calling
you to be.

Amen,
B.Wilder

Fake It Til You Make It

After the facade is over, what were your plans?
It was almost like I was a part of your sick ass
agenda or maybe it was a checklist
Be funny (check)
Show her alot of attention (check)
Make her think I'm serious (check)
Act like I actually have something going for
myself (check)
Make her fall madly in love with me (check)
Then watch everything that you created unravel
right before my eyes
I was tricked, hoodwinked, and bamboozled.
This wouldn't be like the times before with the
cheating and abuse.
No, this would be far worse than all of that
combined.
You would truly fake it til you make it and
destroy my big, genuine heart in the process.
I remember calling on God so many times
because inside my head nothing was right.
I would imagine running you over with my car.
Then check back into reality before stepping on
the gas.
I guess I just wanted to hurt you the same if not
worse than how you hurt me.

My prayer for you is that you are not bitter after
being done wrong by someone. I pray that you
seek understanding and forgiveness through
God. I pray that you recognize there are certain
things that only God can help you with. These
are the sensitive matters of the heart that only
God can help heal. My biggest prayer is that you
get the lessons out of this situation and that you
are able to apply the lesson to your life. That you
soften your heart to forgive and let go of all the
hurt and pain. So that you can finally walk into a
new season to manifest the things you really
want out of life. I pray that your remember God
is always closest to the brokenhearted and he
will never leave you.

Amen,
B. Wilder

Physically Separated, but Emotionally Connected

It makes me sick to my stomach that you still
have a spot in my heart that you never earned
nor deserved, but a spot that you stole.

You played around with my heart, lied and acted
like you were who you said you were, but all
you did was play a role.

Don't pretend that for one second you feel the
same way I do about you.

When you and I both know that's the furthest
thing from true.

I gave genuinely, honestly, and the real me.

I never held back or lied because that's not what
I wanted our relationship to be.

Since day one, all I wanted was a bond like I've
never had.

You forced a fake narrative on me and that's the
reason I'm so damn mad.

Now you have to deal with the karma that comes
with all you did and that is sad.

My prayer for you is that you utilize the spirit of
discernment with people who want to be
connected to you romantically. That you take
things slow and allow them to show their truest
selves to you. That you listen to your spirit when
something doesn't feel right and that you speak
up about what you are feeling. I want you to
know how damaging it can be to be connected to
someone who is not worthy of the love you give.
I pray that if you do end up with someone like
this that you find the strength to rebuild your self
esteem and your relationship with yourself. My
biggest prayer is that you know that God and the
Universe wants you to be happy so keep
believing this and watch as great things start to
happen for you. Breakups can be true blessings
in disguise. My prayer is that after the initial
heartbreak you see the blessings and how these
things are not working against you ,but are
working for you.

Amen,
B.Wilder

I'm Giving Up, Love

You gave your all ,but you were involved in the
unexpected.

Once again left alone and feeling depressed.

Feelings building up now it's time to express.

The aching, empty space left after your crime
and the fall.

Yet again I gave you the key to my heart and you
were selfish in taking it all.

My faith has been tampered with because I was
left in your care.

Now what's my next move?

Everything I do is another scare.

I find myself yelling...How could you?...Why
would you?......What have I ever done?

Yeah I yell your name and hope that things will
go back the same.

But then I realize I've gone too far and there's no
going back.

Damn Love why'd you have to do me like that?

After all the heart aching pain and drowning in
my own tears.

Any person would give up on Love for years.

My biggest prayer is that hurt and pain never
lead you to a place where you give up on love.
That you still keep a glimmer of hope for finding
the love of your life. I pray you believe in being
worthy and deserving of REAL LOVE. That you
don't get so discouraged by people who honestly
were never meant to be that close to you in the
first place. I pray you find the courage to push
past your fears when the right one finds you and
begins to pursue you. My hope is that you rely
on your connection with God to confirm that it is
a divine connection you have. That you don't
move forward until there is clarity and peace
from God when concerning that person.I pray

you walk right into a beautifully, loving, and
fulfilling love that is long lasting.

Amen,
B.Wilder

Rhythmic Quality Time

Midnight,Evening, when our quality time
begins.

and doesn't end,

until 3 in the morning.

Clenching my soul with B flats and C minors.

Creating unexplainable emotions deep within.

Angelic voices ranging from bold bass to soft
sopranos.

Rhythmic pulses fit for a sensual slow dance.

Tones darker than the memory of your first
heartbreak.

Dynamics change our pattern of breathing.

Polyphonic textures create a sense of
independence in harmony.

A sense of connection for the two to become
one.

To pause a musical addiction until passion is
done.

My prayer for you is that your next love story
makes you feel like you are at the concert of
your favorite artist. That seeing the face of your
lover gives you the burning desire to sing.I pray
that their heart sings a melody that only your
heart understands. That being with them is like
hearing that one song that you continuously put
on repeat. My only hope is that spending time
with them is like when you perform your
favorite songs in front of the mirror with your
hairbrush as your microphone. That your love is
fresh, fun, and exciting. I'm praying for a
musically inspired love for you forever.

Amen,
B.Wilder

I Had a Vision of Love

I took a deep breath, prayed to God, closed my eyes, and when I opened them he appeared in my vision:

Standing at a tall 6'2 height

Beautiful chocolate skin

Athletic body with defined muscles

Owning the most gorgeous smile I've ever seen

With the deepest, baritone voice I've ever heard

Smelling of Soft Musk and Sandalwood

Feeling safe, secure, and like my personal protector

With a bright and charming personality

Giving me an experience from a true southern gentleman

Speaking about God because they have a 1-on-1 personal relationship.

Gifted Spiritually and Physically.

He is business minded, a natural go-getter.

Staying super considerate of me throughout all situations.

A generous giver in all aspects of life.

Trustworthy and honest by default.

Fully engaged in just the very thought of me.

Compliments me until I blush like a little schoolgirl.

When I snapped out of my daydream, I couldn't stop crying.God knows the desires of our hearts. I knew that he was real and would be mine one day soon.

My prayer for you is that you know that God doesn't just give us these visions just for sport. He gives us a glimpse into our future of our happiest times. Then later on when we manifest that exact moment ,we claim it's deja vu when it is simply God's promises coming to pass. I pray you trust that what you see and feel in those visions are real and that seeing and feeling it in your vision is just as real as seeing and feeling the real thing to the unconscious mind. I pray that you remember these visions and write them down for they are beautiful blessings from God that belong to you. I pray that God gives you each and every desire of your heart and that it leads you to the happiest days of your life. My biggest prayer is that you get real intentional about your mindset and the thoughts you carry in your mind.

Amen,
B.Wilder

A Simple Reciprocation

He feels just like home.
I've never been so comfortable
Never been so ecstatic
I didn't know that love like this was possible

This must be the type of love Keyshia was
screaming about at the top of her lungs,
Or what made Beyonce and them want to cater.
I tell you, I want you to give me all my love up
front
,but you love to tell me to save some love for
later.

You bring the feminine, soft woman out of me.
I really love it here with you too.
This has got to be how Alicia felt when she sang
If I ain't got you.

There is no way to truly explain what is going
on inside,
of my heart when you are on my mind.
I can identify with Lauryn when she said it was
the sweetest thing she's ever known.
You make me so weak in the knees like SWV,
when I hear your voice on my phone.

How'd you manage to make me fall?
Now there's no way to shake me at all.
Just like Monica, I have your love all over me.
I'm committed to you and there's no other place
I'd rather be.

My prayer is that you find someone who is safe
enough to let your guard down and fully fall.
That they are so open and honest that it is easy
to love them. I pray for an easy and amazing
love like one you've never known.I'm praying
when you ask God if this person is for you, he
says "Absolutely." My biggest prayer is that all
those love songs make sense to you now that
you've experienced a special type of love. I hope
that your deep love that you have always had
inside of you is finally reciprocated instantly. I
pray you never have to beg for anyone to love
you ever again.

Amen,
B.Wilder

AGAPE

Can't shake the feeling.

The feelings of pure joy that it doesn't matter
what I do, or what I don't do and you will never
love me any less.

The love you feel for me is far from conditional.

You're so patient with me when I continue to
hurt you by hurting myself.

You pick me up off the floor and dry my tears
after another failed situationship.

You'd tell me I was worthy all along and to take
my time and wait for who you personally send.

Then What do I do?

Continue to try to make the ones who you
warned me about "The One."

I continuously fall for the tricks of the enemy
and he knows that "love" is exactly how to get
me.

But you, you believe in me.

You know my heart literally.

You knew I was your property,

When I was still a thought in my mother's head.

It's true that I haven't had anything in this life come easy, but even still God your light shines brightly on me.

My prayer for you is that you STOP BEING HARD ON YOURSELF! Give yourself some grace and then give yourself even more than before. Love yourself and speak to yourself the way that you speak to the people that you love. I pray that you understand that you are going to make mistakes because that is part of life. God knows you are going to make the mistakes before you even make them. All you have to do is be honest about it and learn from it. Don't keep making the same mistakes over and over again when God is showing you what to do to get it right this time. Doing that will only cause more heartache and feelings of defeat. God wants you to be the victor and overcome your struggles and strongholds. My biggest prayer is that you know how powerful you are in God. Don't be too afraid or ashamed to ask for help. God wants to do nothing more than help you get through the tough times. Trust him and know that if something is being taken from you it's because God has a plan to replace it with something even better.

Amen,
B.Wilder

G.O.D. over EVERYTHING

Relationship over Religion
Connection over Chaos
Alignment over Anxiety
Favor over Fear
Grace over Grief
Love over Lack
Mercy over Mistakes
Anointing over Arrogance
Elevation over Eagerness
Gifted over Gloating
Authenticity over Acting
Truth over Trauma
Healthy Soul Ties over Toxic Soul Ties
God over Everything

My prayer is that God gets precedents over everything in your life. That you steer clear of making people, places, or things your idols. Praying that you see the positive side of things and always keep faith that you are right where you are supposed to be at any given moment. I pray you learn to trust in God's timing for the timeline of your life. There are many things we want right now that we may not be ready for. So instead of God giving them to us when we want it, we have to work out some things in our characteristics,personalities, minds, or hearts that could turn our blessing into a burden. My hope and prayer is that you find comfort and peace in your timeline even if God has to slow it down.

Amen,
B.Wilder

Grateful God

I may have gone left when you said go right.

Moved forward on something when you told me to stop.

Where I was supposed to wait for your voice and confirmation, I jumped the gun and did it anyway.

Then there are other times that I thought I knew what was better for me and did that instead of listening to you.

God I have disobeyed you so many times.

Thought I could really make things fit my own agenda.

Until I finally realized that the ONLY agenda is yours, Lord.

No matter how hard I try to make things happen, if it is of your will then it will be and if it is not then I have witnessed you perform miracles to keep me and my heart safe.

I've been on the receiving end of rejection being protection.

I have seen how quickly things can change if I put myself in a situation where I could do more damage to myself than healing.

No matter what I did or didn't do, You still love me and give me your unconditional, Agape Love.

Your grace is so sufficient and I am grateful for being a consistent recipient of it.

My prayer for you is that you recognize that God's will is so much better than our own. We tend to think that we know exactly what it is that we want. So when we don't get it, it is heartbreaking. The entire time, God knew it wasn't for you and has something so much better for you. I pray that you are confident in the fact that if God took it away, then he has something bigger and better for you ALWAYS. I pray you trust where God is taking you in this life. Know that a lot of times our purpose is connected to our greatest love story. Sometimes God is pushing us to find our purpose first and the love will come with it. My biggest prayer is that you lean into what God is doing in your life and that you understand you have so much grace.

Amen,
B.Wilder

www.ingramcontent.com/pod-product-compliance
Lightning Source LLC
LaVergne TN
LVHW050933200726
843508LV00011B/2335